Note on Cover Photo

Cover Photo Credit: MICHEL HERSON www.photography bymichel.net
Used by permission.

In 2016 my husband, Dave, and I visited the Portland Japanese Garden where Dave took a photo of some stair steps leading to an undefined destination. We both loved this photo since it reminded us of our first home in Japan in 1956. For the last few years, Dave's photo served as his screen saver. We saw it often and chatted about it. I thought about using it for the cover of this book. However, after Dave's death in 2021, we could not find it.

On the Portland Japanese Garden website, I found Michel Herson's photo which seemed similar to Dave's. It conveys the impression that the pathway to the end of life can be full of beautiful experiences like gratitude, peace, and love. Thank you, Michel Herson, for contributing your photo to this book.

LOOKING FORWARD

Discovering the Art of Dying Well

JACQUELINE McMAKIN

LOOKING FORWARD
DISCOVERING THE ART OF DYING WELL

iUniverse books may be ordered through booksellers or by contacting:

iUniverse
1663 Liberty Drive
Bloomington, IN 47403
www.iuniverse.com
844-349-9409

ISBN: 978-1-6632-4082-8 (sc)
ISBN: 978-1-6632-4083-5 (e)

Library of Congress Control Number: 2022910436

Print information available on the last page.

iUniverse rev. date: 07/19/2022

DEDICATION

This book is dedicated to my mother, Virginia Christman Straub. You were the greatest booster, not only of me, but of everyone in the family, our friends, and anyone who crossed your doorstep. You thought the best of us even though you may not have understood every turn in the road we took. Even now, you continue to cheer us on.

THE STORY OF
LOOKING FORWARD

Discovering the Art of Dying Well

The author and her family were totally unprepared for the terminal diagnosis of their beloved mother and grandmother in 1981. The last year together contained moments of gratitude and much preventable suffering. Questions were triggered: Is there such a thing as dying well? Are there ways to prepare for that? *Looking Forward* is an accessible, encouraging set of stories about the author's quest for answers and those who offered insight, guidance, and support. A handy booklist and reflection questions are included to stimulate your own exploration of this important topic.

APPRECIATION FOR
LOOKING FORWARD

Congratulations and hooray for your work on the topic of dying and writing about it in such an accessible way. Sharing it with others is a gift. You have given me things to think about, to ponder, and to share with family.

Allie Stickney, CEO (retired), Wake Robin
Retirement Community, Shelburne, Vermont.

I hope *Looking Forward* will be widely distributed; it is a short read with veins of gold. It is upbeat and written with humility. Most approaches to death planning are disease-focused. *Looking Forward* applies to everyone in every situation.

Zail S. Berry, MD, MPH, Geriatrics and Palliative
Medicine Physician, Burlington, VT

The easy-to-read format is carried along by your interesting story. It is all there, in just a few pages! I plan to share a Blue Book of my own with my children and encourage them to create one of their own.

Barbara Werle, Hospice Nurse, Shelburne, Vermont.

I began reading it with my pastor hat on, but quickly placed my parent and son hat on top of that! My wife's mother is in hospice care now. Three of our four parents have chronic and terminal diagnoses. Thank you for your clear, concise, personal, and practical guide.

> Rev. Kevin Goldenbogen, Senior Pastor, Charlotte
> Congregational Church, Charlotte, Vermont

Looking Forward is a beautiful, informative, thought-provoking, and insightful gift to people of all ages (including me)! You put into words what many of us struggle to know how to approach, and you do so in a way that is both practical and comforting. WONDERFUL! I have many people I would like to share this with already. It is invaluable, inviting, encouraging, and empowering! Such a beautiful contribution.

> Marilee J. Aronson, Licensed Clinical
> Psychiatrist, Washington DC

Looking Forward is an impressive and beautiful book. It's concise and easily digestible with a lovely and moving mix of story and important ideas. Both reassuring and instructive in a personal style, it covers key bases to consider when thinking about a meaningful final chapter.

> Fran Stoddard, Media Interviewer and Producer,
> "Across the Fence", WCAX, Burlington, Vermont.

WOW! That was a beautiful read. I'd like to talk about this. Also I would like to share it with a group trying to form a Hospice Network. Your words would open a lot of important conversations.

Mark Gabel, UVM Health Center Hospice
Volunteer, Colchester, Vermont.

I just love how you have organized this exploration for yourself and how you were able to convey your insights so clearly and warmly. It seems a perfect roadmap for this crazy journey we are on.

Carol Snow, Hospice Chaplain, Charlotte, Vermont

I plan on using this with my daughter. I think in the not-too-distant future that physicians will be more ready to listen to the wishes of the dying and understand that it is not just about curing and keeping folks alive as long as possible.

Peg MacWilliams, Realtor (Retired)
West Yarmouth, Massachusetts

I absolutely love the format and tone of *Looking Forward*. By leading with your curiosity and with questions you asked yourself, you offer a warm invitation for readers to engage with death and preparing for it.

Mike Young, Executive Director, Hope and
A Home (retired), Washington, DC

Using your book, *Looking Forward*, we have contemplated our own preparation for death and have presented our written intentions to each of our children. Thank you for the nudge to think about, record, and share with family our end-of-life journey.

Jini and Jed Hornung, Educator and Financial
Consultant (retired), Shelburne, Vermont

I am going to use this book to speak with my daughter who is my Executor, both to give her information and also to tell her things I want and don't want surrounding death. Your book was a needed impetus to have this conversation. Also, I want to share it with our Couples Group. We read *Being Mortal* by Atul Gawande. Everyone appreciated that book so much. Your book seems like a natural follow-up.

Sally Dowling, Licensed Mental Health
Counselor (retired), Gaithersburg, Maryland

You have done an amazing job making a topic many would rather avoid interesting, informational, and non-threatening. You have been able to bring theory down to the level of practice. The genius of *Looking Forward* for me is the organization/presentation. You told the story of your own search for a better way of dying after your mother's death by telling the stories of others and sharing the questions they raised for you. The search for your answers to those questions made it into a kind of adventure and gave a structure to disparate ideas. The questions you left up to the reader are thought provoking. It feels like a very easy read, but I think readers will be left with lots to ponder and some next steps to take.

Ricci Waters, Annandale, Virginia

We received your sixteen stories relating to death and preparations for it. Excellent ideas, well worded, worth saving, and reading over and over. We had never really discussed the ramifications of this. We had tried but never quite 'broken the ice' before. Last night we did.

Bob Straub, Author's Brother, Baltimore, Maryland

TABLE OF CONTENTS

INTRODUCTION

Death happens to us all. It evokes different feelings. Death experiences have been beautiful, anguished, welcome, intimate, lonely. All of these words could describe my mother's death in 1981. Since that time I have learned that it is possible to influence the quality of our dying, to tilt toward the positive.

We cannot deny the fact that bodies deteriorate. How we experience that decline is largely up to us. There are choices: to laugh, ignore, resist, learn, communicate, make this time special. It's up to us really. Not the doctor or the family or our loved ones. Sure, they have roles to play. But only we can decide where our primary energy will go – toward being passive, letting developments unfold, or being creative, choosing who will accompany us and what our focus will be.

The stories in this collection describe some of the people who came to my aid during and after my mother's death. They offered insights, tools and presence. Out of that abundance, I have selected fifteen "a ha's" that opened doors and made me happy.

What is offered here are my discoveries as a healthy person contemplating my eventual decline and death. People who face the death of a child or of someone suffering the effects of a serious illness or accident or the sudden unexpected death of a person before their time face unique challenges that are not addressed directly here.

There is much to learn about dying well. I have been gathering tips for a long time. At first, I thought of sharing them in the form of a handbook or toolkit. But that didn't feel right. "To Do" lists can weigh us down. Also I don't want to be in the position of suggesting what others should do about such a personal matter as death. Sharing my own stories seemed to be the way to go.

I'm hoping these short pieces highlight the benefits of preparation and the help that is available for those who are contemplating their own death or wish to do so. This is not an exhaustive list of ways to prepare. It does not include some of the practical aspects like filling out Advanced Directives. That would be too much.

Illumination starts with a good question. I have shared some of the questions that came to me and what happened when I gave them attention. I hope this encourages you to focus on your own questions and to search for insights that make sense for you.

Jackie McMakin
Shelburne, Vermont
2022

1

INTO THE HANDS OF ANGELS

In 1977, Josefina Magno shared her dream of establishing a hospice in Northern Virginia. An oncologist and palliative care doctor, she had visited hospices in England and totally embraced the hospice purpose: to help people die with dignity, without pain, in a warm home-like setting surrounded by those called to companion the dying.

In June, 1980, my mother was diagnosed with lung and brain cancer. Living in New Rochelle, New York with my father, she was treated by doctors in a New York City hospital. I offered to stay with them. "Oh, no," they said. "We're in good hands."

But they were not. Things went downhill quickly. My normally attractive and vivacious mother was looking horrible. The doctors assured me she was responding well to the medicine. That was not true.

Finally, I couldn't stand the situation. I wanted Jo's vision of compassionate hospice care for my mother. It was unavailable in New York at the time. On one of my monthly visits from our home in Northern Virginia, I asked Mom if she would like to come and visit us. She readily agreed.

My husband, Dave, outfitted our screened porch with a mattress for us so Mom could have our bedroom. She settled in happily. The next day the hospice doctor and nurse visited. I can't recall anything the visitors said. What was unforgettable was their gentle, reassuring, knowledgeable manner. Soon Mom was enrolled in hospice home care. It was like being delivered into the hands of angels. The hospice team coached us every step of the way and could always make things more bearable or comfortable.

Mom loved being around our daughter, Peg, our exchange student, Judy, our son, Tom, and his friend, Barry, when they were home from college. Even though her cancer could not be stopped, she was happy living with us supported by the hospice team. She slipped away on June 5, 1981.

It was through Shirley Du Boulay's biography *Cicely Saunders: The Founder of the Modern Hospice Movement* that I gained a deeper understanding of hospice. Cicely Saunders, as she trained in London after World War II, to be a nurse, social worker and then a doctor, worked in hospitals and was drawn to being with dying people. She listened to patients' stories and used their ideas to envision the kind of care that would bring peace and dignity to their last days. Du Boulay describes Saunders' regular visits with three dying friends, "chatting, gossiping, telling them about her dream of one day building a hospice." The friends prayed for her and contributed ideas.

Cicely Saunders

Consulting patients and learning their wisdom was foundational for the new hospice Saunders envisioned. Patients were her primary teachers. Staff members were expected to spend generous amounts of time with each patient mutually sharing hopes and dreams, as equals, bound in a fellowship of "two-way giving." This is what we sensed with my mother's hospice team. Each one was a person first and treated Mom and us as persons. They never seemed to be in a hurry and were available twenty-four hours a day. That was terrifically reassuring.

Cicely Saunders envisioned her hospice staff as a "community, united by a strong sense of vocation with a great diversity of outlook in a spirit of freedom." We felt this with Mom's hospice team – they were a community of people who were deeply called to work with dying people. They saw this work as a special privilege.

Saunders' study of physical suffering taught her techniques that would keep patients pain-free and alert. In New York, Mom had experienced terrible discomfort. It was awful for her and us. With Hospice, she was comfortable, peaceful, and able to enjoy being read to by the children.

Many people still have the mistaken idea that if ill people enroll in hospice, they are giving up. I see it differently. For me, it is a chance to be with people who are uniquely trained and totally dedicated to making the dying time special.

Being with hospice freed us to focus on the good things.

2

⌒·⫶·⌒

PASSING IT ON –
THE BLUE BOOK

It was Ted Pockman's turn to lead our support and learning group, a cadre of people who met regularly for personal support and growth. At one of our gatherings, Ted showed us a notebook, describing it as a "how to" manual for his son. "When I'm incapacitated in some way, this tells Will all he needs to know about handling our affairs."

Ted Pockman

Ted said a few words about each section covering legal, financial, practical, and personal matters. A free flowing discussion followed. Dave and I were impressed. "This is what we want to do for our kids," we said afterwards. It was so sensible and needed.

We asked Ted for a copy of his Table of Contents. Then Dave went to work creating sections for my review, feedback and editing. We put copies of the completed pages in three blue notebooks, one for us and each of our two kids. Christened the Blue Book, it has been called that ever since. Here is the Table of Contents we started with (and have updated as information changed over time):

A. Legal

- Trusts and Wills
- Advance Directives for Jackie and Dave

B. Assets

- Net Worth
- Mutual Funds
- Income
- Valuables
- Insurance

C. Business (details on the family real estate business Dave managed at the time)
D. Household Finance
E. Home
F. Passwords
G. Medical and Vital Data

H. Death

- Whom to inform
- The executor process
- Remembrance ritual

I. Reflections and Thoughts

How would the kids react when presented with the Blue Book? They were delighted and wanted to share it with friends! This happened when we were in our sixties. The Blue Book was a door opener to many illuminating family discussions about death. The kids had a playlist for what they would need to do upon our demise or incapacity. We are happy we got this done. So are Tom and Peg.

3

A BEAUTIFUL GUIDE TO HEALING

After Mom died, I was angry with cancer. How could this disease demolish my beautiful, engaging, wonderful mother? For a long time, if I heard someone had cancer, I'd run in the opposite direction and hide.

Then my friend, Sally Dowling, gave me *Kitchen Table Wisdom: Stories That Heal* (1994), by Rachel Remen, a pediatrician and psychotherapist. Her book presents stories of people facing cancer in a way that brought healing, communion, and compassion. The cancer did not disappear, but healing came. How so?

Rachel Remen

For Rachel Remen, there is a huge difference between healing and curing. This was a new idea for me. In an interview with Bill Moyers, she said, "Healing is a process we're all involved in all the time...it is the leading forth of wholeness in people...People have been healing each other long before there were doctors." In a note, Dr. Remen added, "Basically, cure is not always possible...but healing is."

Through the Commonweal Cancer Help Program in California, Remen and her colleagues have offered opportunities for participants to listen deeply to their own truth, then to write it down as simply as possible, and finally, if so moved, to share it with others. "We don't fix things or offer solutions," she told Moyers. "We just listen."

Doctors in Remen's generation were not trained to offer open-ended listening. Their commitment was to cure illness and save lives. If this were impossible, most doctors did not learn ways to handle that within themselves and with patients.

As I read Rachel's stories, several things happened within me. I realized some of my anger was toward my mother's New York doctors. When they heard I was taking Mom to live with our family in Virginia, they objected to my removing her from hospital care and exposing our family to her physical decline and ultimate death. I was also angry with Mom's friends whose facial expressions when visiting reminded me of Edvard Munch's famous painting "The Scream". My mother did not need to see their shock even though it was real and understandable.

Dr. Remen's books showed how ill equipped my mother's New York doctors and friends were to express affection and caring in the midst of suffering. Not being able to cure Mom, the doctors did not know what to do. It would have been better if they had said that cure was not possible and acknowledged how hard that was for them and us.

Slowly, my upset with these doctors and friends morphed into understanding and forgiveness. I began to see how difficult it was for people without training and experience to express caring for those facing the end.

"There's a healthy way to have a disease, a way to use this difficult experience to come to know more intimately who we are and what is important to us," Rachel Remen writes in *My Grandfather's Blessing: Stories of Strength, Refuge, and Belonging* (2000). In addition to being a physician, almost seventy years ago she became chronically ill with Crohn's Disease. This she has found to be her most powerful and intimate teacher. "I have accompanied many people as they have discovered in themselves an unexpected strength, a courage beyond what they would have thought possible, an unsuspected sense of compassion, or a capacity for love deeper than they had ever dreamed. I have watched people abandon values that they have never questioned before and find the courage to live in new ways."

If there is a healthy way to have a disease and to care for those who are ill, I wanted to learn how to practice it.

When it comes to my own diminishment and decline, I would like Rachel Remen, through her stories, by my side, a beautiful, knowledgeable guide to making the end time meaningful for me and those who are with me. When I read her books, it is like she is talking with me, personally present in the room, gently describing a healthy way to go.

4

FINDING MY OWN PATH

A doctor friend, Arnold Golodetz, learned he had a terminal illness. Living in an assisted living community, he described his options in a short essay for its annual literary magazine. Here's an excerpt: "Post-operatively, the surgeon bestowed on me my new status – cancer person ... What do I want – a 'tame' death or a 'wild' one? ... I must think out my own path to 'tame.'"

Arnold and Virginia Golodetz

Arnold had picked up the terms "wild" and "tame" from a book by Phillippe Aries called *The Hour of Our Death*. For Arnold, "tame" meant a death congenial with his values.

I admired Arnold's decision to say "no" to what his oncologist described as "treatment" and what he saw as "poisons for my malevolent rebel cells."

What did Arnold's essay tell me? He was finding a path to dying on his own terms. I wanted to learn from him. "How can I help my friend who is struggling with pancreatic cancer?" I asked. His response stunned me with its clarity:

- It's important to know one's own thinking about death, what matters most.
- Have some way to deal with the fear associated with dying.
- Figure out how to deal with the medical establishment's propensity to focus on cure rather than care.
- Have a circle of intimates to be with you so death is not solitary.

"It's a journey," he said. "Decisions need to be made, but be flexible. Things could change. A decision made now might not be a good one as time goes by."

Afterwards I realized that I wanted to clarify my own thinking about death. With Arnold's points in mind, I started writing. Here's an excerpt:

"In facing my own death, my thoughts cluster around these words:

- Conscious – I'd like to be awake, accepting of death's many facets as well as my own and other people's responses.
- Courage – I want to be open to all aspects – completion, separation, pain, peace, letting go, the feeling that I'm done and others are not.
- Communion – I'd like a union of hearts with God and others – this can continue.
- Comfort – I'd like giving and receiving, holding, touch, music, singing."

The process of writing was illuminating. It was lovely to follow in Arnold's footsteps to think through my own path to "tame". My Philosophy of Death, as I called it, was produced ten years ago. It makes me happy when I read it. It is an anchor.

5

A NEW FRIEND
SHOWS THE WAY

Seemingly out of the blue one day, Arnold said, "I would like you to meet my doctor." This was Zail Berry, a palliative care consulting physician. Arnold died before a meeting could be arranged. Did his dying process go the way he had envisioned? I wondered. After his death, I phoned Zail and mentioned that Arnold had wanted to introduce us. Soon after, we met, shared our experiences with Arnold, and began a discussion of factors that contribute to dying well. Eventually, Zail led a workshop on this for our community. Here are some key points from that event.

Zail Berry

Dying well takes preparation. "A good death is one that happens with qualities such as peace, comfort, expressions of love, healing of relationships, meaningful interaction with others. Uncontrolled pain, anxiety and depression prevent one from experiencing a good death. Palliative care maximizes the possibility of a person dying well. This rarely happens in a good way without forethought."

My curiosity was peaked. How does one prepare? What is palliative care?

Dying well involves personal connection. Zail related a story she had read in *The Washington Post* about a mother of young children who knew her death was coming. Calling together friends and acquaintances, she shared the kind of help that would be needed. Those gathered divided the tasks, carried them out, and walked with her to the end. After her death, a reporter interviewed the group. Everyone said what a gift it was to have been part of that team, how special it was to be bonded around a shared purpose, and how sorry they were not to still be part of it. Zail drew this conclusion: "Asking for help with your dying experience is a gift you can give to others."

This made perfect sense. But I was new to Vermont at the time, knew no one really well, and was left wondering, "Whom could I ask for help?"

Dying well is strengthened when it is part of a community that supports it. "Are there ways a community could set up structures that would strengthen our ability to help each other with end of life matters? Could a community create a model that would deal with this well?"

Zail's questions set a firecracker under me. How DO you create a model that would deal with death well? Where are these models? Who is doing a good job of this? What can we learn from them? I decided to find out.

6

WHO'S IN CHARGE?

Being Mortal: Medicine and What Matters at the End (2014) was an instant bestseller. Its author, surgeon and professor of medicine Dr. Atul Gawande, focuses on what medicine has to offer the dying and their families. His regrettable conclusion:

Atul Gawande

The problem with medicine and the institutions it has spawned for the care of the sick and the old is not that they have had an incorrect view of what makes life significant. The problem is that they have had almost no view at all...Medical professionals concentrate on repair of health, not sustenance of the soul ... Yet this is the painful paradox – we have decided that they should be the ones who largely define how we live in our waning days.

In his book, Gawande weaves the stories of the deaths of his father and his wife's grandmother, Alice Hobson. Gawande's father, at life's end, found moments worth living for – having dinner parties, making plans for the college in India that he helped start, sending out emails, watching films with his wife.

Alice, as her health declined, loved her friends, privacy, and had a purpose to her days until her family moved her to a senior living complex. This reassured the family but not Alice: "It involved the imposition of more structure and supervision than she'd ever had to deal with before. She didn't like being nannied or controlled."

This question emerged for me from Gawande's book:

Who is in charge in our waning years?

Dr. Gawande's father was able to keep making his own decisions to the end. Alice started out that way. Then her family took over. After she was enrolled, the institution took charge. And what about the doctor? Many hope that the

♦

19

doctor will know what to do and guide them through the process. Gawande: "You don't have to spend much time with the elderly or those with terminal illness to see how often medicine fails the people it is supposed to help." Gawande's first sentence in the book is an honest admission: "I learned about a lot of things in medical school, but mortality wasn't one of them."

On the job, Gawande learned what people really want: "People don't ask for much, only to keep shaping the story of their life in the world – to make choices and sustain connections to others according to their own priorities."

Yes!!! I thought. For as long as possible, **I want to be in charge!** I want to think through my own choices, maintain contact with people with whom I have a real connection and be clear about my priorities.

In the fifteenth century, written guides to the art of dying or *ars moriendi* were popular. Their advice: accept death calmly; hope only for God's forgiveness; let go of possessions; ponder questions; know prayers that have sustained others; consider your final words.

If I am to be in charge of how I respond to life's end, I'd like a written guide. I need to pull together in one place those understandings and prayers that most sustain my soul. No one else can do this for me.

7

SLOW DEATH

"Slow death" is a concept I hadn't thought much about until I read Stephen Kiernan's book *Last Rights: Rescuing the End of Life from the Medical System* (2006). Most deaths used to be relatively sudden. Now, with medical advances, Kiernan points out, we can keep people alive longer. Slow death has become the norm. There is an advantage to this. It gives us time to prepare and ennoble the end of life.

Like Dr. Gawande, Kiernan notes that for many people, dying is largely a medical experience in the hospital or nursing home where the focus is to prolong life and doctors are ill equipped to help patients pass time in a fulfilling way. He calls for a different model:

Stephen Kiernan

- doctors who offer simple presence, listening, and symptom relief and are cautious in recommending treatments and tests that may have dubious value;
- families who make the most of the time they have and do not put loved ones through medical ordeals to buy time;
- patients who focus on the opportunity to be thoughtful in the dying process rather than submitting to pressure to prolong life.

Kiernan compares the experiences of birth and death. "A baby is born into a community." Parents, grandparents, and friends bring food, share stories, help with driving. Death is different. "Too often life's end is also its loneliest phase." People don't know how to relate.

He imagines another path:

- a dying person remains in a community until his or her last breath;
- a health system helps families who need care and an understanding of their role;
- professionals and families join forces and find support in the community.

The term "slow death" made me sit up and take notice. For the last eight years, I have visited and led singing each week with the residents in the health care section of our retirement community. I know slow death very well. It can last twenty years, as it did for Mary. It can cut you off from conversation with family and friends because of total hearing loss, as it had for Paul. It can cause you to trundle with your walker incessantly around the circle of the memory care unit and prevent you from recognizing your own kids, as it did for Ginny.

Reading Kiernan's book, I was left with questions: How do I ennoble the end of life? How can I do that when I'm well? And.....how long a life do I want? When life's systems begin to shut down, do I want to hang on as long as others can keep me going?

8

ACTIONS ONLY I CAN TAKE

In college I learned that each phase of human development has a task. Children learn the basics, teens discover their own voice and separate from parents, adults do work that provides for family and contributes to society.

It is Dr. Ira Byock, palliative care physician and teacher, who has championed the idea that dying has its own development tasks. Physical decline can be accompanied by emotional and spiritual expansion, connection and communion. Dying does not only have to be passive; there are actions I can take that offer peace and possibility for growth. What are they?

Ira Byock

In his book, *Dying Well: Peace and Possibilities at the End of Life* (1997), Dr. Byock elucidates:

> *I have met a number of people who were emotionally well, while their physical body was withering... Even as they are dying, most people can accomplish meaningful tasks and grow in ways that are important to them and to their families ... I began keeping notes on the development landmarks and 'taskwork' ... relevant to the end of life ... I hope that naming the taskwork might provide paths for a person's individual journey.*

Items on Dr. Byock's list include:

- worldly affairs: leaving practical matters in good order for others to take over;
- legacy: figuring out what to leave behind that would enhance others;

- completion of relationships: expressing regret, seeking reconciliation, saying thanks, offering words and gestures of love;
- making peace with reality: letting go of independence and relationships;
- transcendence: opening to the mystery and sense of awe available in dying.

In his book *Four Things That Matter Most,* Dr. Byock shows how transforming it can be to address these "four things":

- "Please forgive me."
- "I forgive you."
- "Saying thanks"
- "I love you."

Dying, according to Byock, creates a unique opening that might not have been possible before to speak about these things. "It shakes us free of the veneers, the layers of personality, of who we think we are, of protecting ourselves... it really wakes us from ...[the] illusion of immortality."

When I read Dr. Byock's thoughts on development tasks for dying, I was elated. Here were practical things I could do to prepare well for my death. Stimulated by what Dr. Byock offered, I made up my own list - concrete actions that help me focus on how to complete life in a way that expresses what matters most. Slowly, I am accomplishing these tasks.

During rounds, a resident, noticing Dr. Byock's special gift with dying people, asked, "What's your secret?" He responded, "I think of everyone as being well."

Dr. Byock's reply has been so inspiring. I want to think of others and myself as well even as we are dying.

9

GATHERING TOGETHER

The message from Jim, someone I had not heard from in years, was a jolt: "My first wife, Jane Quinn Gray, is near death from cancer. I thought you would like to know. The entire saga can be found at the CaringBridge website."

Jane Quinn Gray

Logging in, I learned that Jane had died the day before. Reading through the entries, I was struck by how much loving happened through Jane's illness and death. One entry by her daughter, Jeannie, particularly stayed with me:

> *I just got off the phone with Mom – had a great talk. She met one of the nurse practitioners today, and just loved her. The nurse said, "This will be one of the richest times of your life." Mom said, 'It's true – everyone is so unguarded, and really expresses their love, and what they really feel.' She feels so loved and supported.*

One friend offered a poem by Wendell Berry:

> *When I rise up, let me rise up joyfully*
> *like a bird.*
> *When I fall, let me fall without regret*
> *like a leaf, like a leaf.*

Another shared a Celtic prayer:

> *Calm me, O Lord, as you stilled the storm.*
> *Still me, O Lord, keep me from harm.*
> *Let all the tumult within me cease.*
> *Enfold me, Lord, in Your peace.*

All of this was moving. A true community of support formed around Jane, her family and friends through CaringBridge.

I thought back to Mom. Bringing her to Virginia was a good decision under the circumstances. But it did deprive loved ones in New York of communication and presence – not intentionally but because we did not know about services like CaringBridge. When a person dies, there are circles of caring: some people on the inside, others somewhat removed, others far away or even out of touch. Death is a moment when we want to gather together, to be close, even if we don't quite know how. Writing provides a way to express caring. It can be created as the inspiration strikes and read in the recipient's own time. CaringBridge invited us to do that with Jane and her loved ones. Doors opened.

10

A GRACEFUL PASSING

Our associate minister, Susan, and I decided to create a workshop to share death preparation tools that we ourselves had found beneficial. The workshop was experiential. Everyone, including the facilitators, used the tools to create certain "products." Some products were practical like filling out the Advanced Directive form, creating a Table of Contents for each person's "Blue Book", and creating a list of people who might lend support at the end. Others required more reflection like writing a philosophy of death. Susan called our workshop "A Graceful Passing."

Susan Cooke Kittredge

People did some real thinking and digging. I especially liked this piece by Linda:

Please don't leave me to die alone. I've spent 40 to 70% of my life alone and am done with that. As I leave, I would leave the curtains open so you can see the process. Bring me your color, song, and light. Don't be afraid to joke and tell stories. We haven't been taught well how to do respectful privacy, but our humanness should win out over it all, both yours and mine. Too many friends and family members have left without my engagement in their process, respect for privacy being the excuse. Love each other, and don't worry about privacy. In writing this, I fear the medical establishment, pain and loss of freedom in that order. Who knows what it will feel like at death's door? Just come, bring yourself, be yourself, we already have a history.

Reading this I thought, Wow! People are discovering their own insights and getting started with work they want to do. It was useful to have the support of the group for our own explorations.

However, after one or two sessions a few participants left. They had bumped into real obstacles to thinking creatively about their final days. Some were wrestling with painful deaths in their past. One person had become exhausted caring alone as her beloved husband died an agonizing death from cancer.

Even those who remained in the workshop had difficulty finding time to give to it. We concluded that for most people there is rarely a good time when one has space and energy to prepare thoughtfully for one's final days.

I wanted to learn more about how to mobilize energy to prepare for one's death. For this, I turned to my friend, Craig Smith.

11

FAMILY MATTERS

"I'm bothered by those people who left the 'A Graceful Passing' workshop," I told Craig.

"Is there a way to make it easier to do the preparation I know they would like to do?"

An Episcopal priest, Craig Smith is used to helping people deal with death. In addition, he is trained in family systems theory, a way of looking at personal and interpersonal relationships through the lens of family of origin. He replied, "It would probably be good to consider the influence of family."

Craig Smith

We designed a three-session workshop called "Family Matters" to help participants tackle these questions:

- How did the family that raised us deal with death and other transitions?
- What patterns would we like to carry forward from the past?
- How would we want to walk differently with death and transition in the future?

First, participants were invited to create a genogram, a visual map of family relationships and patterns in general. I noticed in my family there were a few close relationships and many distant ones. Also we tended to sweep things under the rug. Lots of topics just were not discussed.

Next, we pondered family patterns related specifically to death and dying. In my family, death was a "no go zone".

As a child, I was not included at family funerals. Deaths were secret, secular, non-participatory and directed by funeral homes.

What alternatives appealed more? I realized I wanted my own dying and final ritual to be open, participatory, spiritual, and created by those who feel called to be with me in my decline. Craig remembered death in his family as a time when family members blessed each other and affirmed the most important stuff. What a wonderful thought! That was what I wanted too.

Our next workshop task was to convert the list of what we wanted at death to intentions that would guide the realization of these dreams. I committed to continue to ponder questions that occurred and hunt for answers. We also were challenged to identify an inner change that might help convert intentions into actions. An inner pattern I wanted to change was preoccupation with "getting things done." Letting go of that would release emotional energy to be more available to whatever presented itself.

At the end of the workshop, I was much more aware of the power of my default operating system from my family of origin: do as little with death as possible! I was energized to deal with death differently - more openly, creatively, and intentionally. That clarity gave me energy to get on with the preparation I wanted to do.

12

A CIRCLE OF INTIMATES

When Arnold Golodetz recommended having a circle of intimates for support at the end of life, the idea was immediately appealing to me. I held this as a wish, but not as a probability. We were new to Vermont and didn't as yet know many people.

But then some unexpected things happened. At a rehearsal of the chorus I had joined, Claudia Rose sat next to me. We felt an instant connection. Claudia is an energy healer. From her I began learning simple and effective techniques for calling forth positive and letting go of negative energy. Sometime after that, in the moments before rehearsal, Claudia asked, "Jackie, when you get ready to leave your body, would you like me to be with you?"

Claudia Smith

You could have picked me up off the floor! "Of course!" I said, "Thank you so much for offering." Another day I asked, "You live so far away, how do you envision being with me in those last days?" "Oh, I would probably visit you once a week at first," she replied. "Toward the end, if it were needed, I could see moving in with you." I was so touched.

After meeting Zail Berry when Arnold died, we continued to see each other. I trusted her palliative care medical expertise and appreciated her warm friendship. When I asked her about the medical aspects of dying, she said she would be there for me at the end. I was thrilled.

Now there were two people in my circle of intimates. It seemed like a miracle!

As I pondered the circle and what might be needed, my thoughts turned to faith. Ever since I first explored spiritual matters as a teenager, the stories and images of the Christian way have fed my soul. I wanted someone in my circle who also had been nourished in the same way. Craig came to mind. We had become soul friends, meeting regularly to share insights and encouragement. He readily agreed to participate. I was so grateful.

Now the circle felt complete. Surprisingly, something else happened. Another choir friend, Mary Catharine Jones, came for lunch after attending the first workshop, "A Graceful Passing." When I mentioned how good it felt to have a circle, she said, "I want to be in your circle too!" Of course, I said yes. "What do you envision bringing to it?" I asked. "Oh, I could make soup or nail down details," she said. A great organizer, she led the first get-together of our group.

Mary Catharine Jones

How happy I am to have these four people available to share thoughts now and to be with me at the end. They feel called to do this. Of course, our son and daughter and I are supporting one another as we age and will continue to do so. It is reassuring that we also have committed care from friends in addition to family.

13

OFF RAMPS

When our Montana family planned to visit over Thanksgiving, Dave and I wanted them to meet Zail Berry. I asked Zail how we should prepare. She said, "Don't do anything. Leave it to me."

We had about an hour for the visit. Zail jumped right in. Addressing our son, Tom, and his wife, Mary, she said, "Your parents will die from one of a number of causes." Possible scenarios included a slow decline as basically healthy people, a catastrophic accident, a rapid or slow decline from serious illness, slow decline with increasing cognitive impairment, and hastening death as a conscious choice by taking an off ramp.

Turning to us all, Zail said, "Think of life as a highway. If you look down the highway and don't like what you see, you can take an off ramp. You need to understand that much of the medical world will be geared toward blocking the off ramps and keeping you alive. It's important to get the support you need and identify where the right exits are for you." This made sense. Arnold had chosen the terminal cancer diagnosis as his off ramp and refused treatment designed to prolong life. Dave and I admired him for it.

Zail continued, "Think about what would trigger someone to take an off ramp." Then she proceeded to give some examples. "You're hit by a car as a healthy person. You survive with mind OK but confined to a nursing home for the rest of life. You could request, 'Don't put me back together' if your future quality of life is not what you want.'" A friend of ours, Kate, had faced this exact choice, and decided to let go. We had supported that decision.

The conversation with Zail was open and frankly encouraging. It was good to have so many insights and scenarios on the table. We were all glad we had met.

When I had a quiet moment after the family left, I sat down at the computer and poured out my thoughts. I posed some questions and opened myself to what I was hearing. I noted the off ramps I would take and the triggers that would move me in a direction. It was clear. Triggers included being so deaf that I was totally isolated from normal conversation, or being so sight impaired that I could not go outside alone. If I am not finished off by a disease or an accident, I would, with my family and circle, decide when to stop eating and drinking.

Voluntary stopping eating and drinking is becoming more known. What inspires me about this option is the idea of letting nature take its course. When I focused on my desire to have as natural a death as possible, this option came to mind. I remembered the Native American custom of elders heading for the desert to await death's coming. If a car is broken, why continue to give it fuel in hopes of coaxing a few more driving miles from it? Why not honor the completion of one's life and welcome death as the natural conclusion? What about moving on so others can take over? What about choosing to use less of the earth's resources to prolong a life that has been completed?

My friend, Jack, a doctor suffering from terminal cancer, decided to let go of life. He had made a list of friends with whom he wanted to say thanks and goodbye. When that was completed, he stopped taking nourishment and drink. A couple of days later when asked how he was doing, he smiled and said, "Fine. Just fine." His only family member, Meg, was at peace, knowing her father had died on his own terms.

Mary and Tom McMakin

14

❧ ✦ ❧

GIVING BIRTH TO A VISION

Observing Jack die on his own terms led me to think more about how dying well would look to me. For inspiration I turned to Henri Nouwen's book *Our Greatest Gift: A Meditation on Caring and Dying* (1994). A tenured professor at Harvard Divinity School, author and priest, Henri Nouwen received a phone call from Jean Vanier, Director of L'Arche, a worldwide community of homes for people who are mentally disabled and their assistants. Vanier asked, "Henri, would you consider becoming pastor-in-residence at our L'Arche home in Toronto?"

Henri Nouwen

It took a year for Nouwen to say yes, to move from the highest intellectual circles to living with people who could not tie their shoes. This transition was his call to "downward mobility." Henri learned that L'Arche residents had as much to teach him about living and dying as he had to share with them.

Moe, a fifty-eight-year-old person with Down's Syndrome, was endowed with a singular capacity to give and receive love. When Moe died, there was a true celebration. Afterwards, Nouwen's fiend asked him, "Where and how do you want to die?" This prompted them to ask themselves:

> *Are we preparing ourselves for our death, or are we ignoring death by keeping busy? Are we helping each other to die, or do we simply assume we are going to always be here for each other? Will our death give new life, new hope, and new faith to our friends, or will it be no more than another cause for sadness?*

On the top floor of a home shared with friends, Nouwen devoted five weeks to pondering these questions and penned what has become one of my favorite books, *Our Greatest Gift: A Meditation on Caring and Dying.*

> *I want to die well (befriend my death)*
> *and also help others to die well.*

Nouwen thought of his sister-in-law, Marina, whose death had blessed those who knew her. Sharing painting and poetry, a direct fruit of her efforts to befriend death, she taught others who were strengthened by her love. Nouwen's discovery:

Our death may be the end of our success, our productivity, our fame, or our importance among people, but it is not the end of our fruitfulness.

This led to the question that shaped his reflections:

How can I live so that I can be fruitful after death?

The idea of bearing fruit even in and after death had power for him. It produced energy and resolve to tackle some of the death preparation he wanted to do.

Nouwen's experience has been helpful as I made his steps my own. I wanted to carve out time to listen to my inner teacher, and write down my thoughts on how dying well would look to me. Soon I would have a chance to do that.

15

~~//~~

BEFRIEND DEATH

Advent is a four-week period in the church year to prepare for the coming of light in the darkness, the birth of Jesus. As Advent approaches, my custom is to ask for a theme to give focus to my preparation. A few years ago, what popped into my head was "befriend death." I decided to focus on these words during the first moments of each weekday and open my heart to any thoughts and ideas that might come.

The words "I will sustain you to the end" were part of the Scripture readings for the first Sunday of Advent. The writer is saying that God will nourish us for the duration and give gifts for the journey. I found that so reassuring.

On Hallowing One's Diminishments is the title of a pamphlet my friend, John Yungblut, had written when coping with Parkinson's Disease. The word "hallowing" means "to make holy, to consecrate, to respect greatly." For John this meant doing "something creative" with his illness and death. Several ways to do this occurred:

- treat diminishments as companions
- maintain a friendly attitude toward them
- exercise a kind of playfulness in relation to them
- recognize that these companions had gifts to offer
- write about them
- meditate on them, listening in silence and noting thoughts that occur

John Yungblut

John's discoveries inspired me to write my own reflections on being creative with death.

It was totally liberating to focus on befriending death. What was my unique way to do this? Only my inner teacher had answers. It was fascinating to hear what this teacher had to say.

This listening and writing was so enlivening that I continued it after Advent was over. The writings, each no more than a page, were like a gift that kept giving. Every time I read one, I am uplifted, reminded of what is true for me. They are pieces written by me for me - my own guide to dying well. I am happy to show them to others, but primarily they are for me. They reinforce how I want to live and respond to the experience of diminishment. They are the notes that enable me to march to my own drummer.

One day I saw my one-hundred-year old friend, Bill, jauntily walking down the road. How we got talking, I don't remember. But his words have endured. "Jackie, when you make peace with dying, you can have fun for the rest of your life." How true!

16

AFTERWORD: PLAN AHEAD

A goofy PLAN AHEAd sign was posted in our home. Clearly the sign writer didn't plan ahead. Planning is on my mind now related to death. We know death cannot be corralled or predicted. The best-laid plans can go awry. However, planning ahead can prevent much unnecessary suffering.

What is offered in these stories are ingredients, not a recipe. They are tools. Each deepened my understanding. Perhaps they might inspire you to notice the ingredients that would enrich your last days.

Many of these tools and ideas came through individuals. I call these people "saints" or "light keepers". Their wisdom illuminates my contemplation of life's conclusion. They have more experience and knowledge than I do. An ancient prayer ends, "At the hour of my death, bid me come to you that with thy saints I may praise you for evermore." Who are light keepers for you?

How to describe the goal we have in mind as we prepare for the end? A good death, dying well, a conscious death? The idea of a "conscious death" came alive when John Yungblut embraced it as his goal. As Parkinson's Disease was getting the better of him, he and his wife, Penelope, discussed what they could do to support John's desire for a conscious death. They defined this as the ability of the person and their companion to recognize that dying is taking place and the willingness to face the issues involved. Penelope prepared their bedroom with some of John's favorite objects on display. Much loved books and readings were assembled. People came to visit and make their goodbyes. They wanted John's blessing. He could give them that.

Penelope Yungblut

After John died, I talked with Penelope about how it went. "It was like a courtship time. There was tremendous sweetness, but at the same time, I felt terrible because I knew we were going to lose him." This conversation with Penelope was so moving. It was the first time I knew a couple who identified conscious dying as their goal and then explored together how that could happen.

What ran through my head when choosing the title *Looking Forward* for these essays? Certainly not saying goodbye to loved ones. And, of course, I'm not looking forward to any suffering. Enlisting creativity related to dying, as John and Penelope did, does appeal. I am looking forward to how that plays out.

My husband, Dave always loved Dr. Oliver Sacks' medical stories. Toward the end of his life, Dr. Sacks wrote four articles on his final journey. These were published in the *New York Times*. Dave placed copies of these essays in a plastic folder, with a Christmas 2015 note for our children:

In our lifetime there have been many giants. Oliver Sacks is one of them, so we thought we would share these essays he wrote at the end of his life. We think Sacks' insights in these essays are worthwhile for all of us no matter where we are on our life journey.

Raised in an Orthodox Jewish family in the outskirts of London, Sacks recalled how the Sabbath was honored: "the Sabbath was entirely different from the rest of the week. No work was allowed, no driving, no use of the telephone; it was forbidden to switch on a light or a stove…"

Oliver Sachs

The day before he died, Oliver Sacks penned these words,

> *I find my thoughts, increasingly, not on the supernatural or spiritual, but on what is meant by living a good and worthwhile life – achieving a sense of peace within oneself. I find my thoughts drifting to the Sabbath, the day of rest, the seventh day of the week, and perhaps the seventh day of one's life as well, when one can feel that one's work is done, and one may, in good conscience, rest.*

Reflecting on my own decline and that of others, I see that life gets simpler. Many of the things we have cared about fall into the background. Finally, we are left with ourselves. Holding things lightly in my hands seems the way to be – letting go into love. And then relaxing into what Oliver Sacks described as, "the Sabbath". Rest.

FOR REFLECTION

What **insights and stories** captured your attention as you read *Looking Forward*? Included also are a number of **tools, practices, and questions** to prepare for and enrich the end of life. Which speak to you? Here's a list:

- Articulate for yourself **your own questions as they arise** about your death; notice answers that come across your path; think about the organ grinder's monkey who holds out a cup for donations; hold out a cup with your own questions; you'll be surprised that pennies drop in (Introduction)

- Get acquainted with **hospice and palliative care** services in your area (Chapter 1)

- Begin preparing a **Blue Book** for those who will finish up your affairs (Chapter 2)

- Collect **nourishing writings or images** (an inspiring poem, photo, phrase, piece of music) that **you want as part of your life's end; who might be a guide for you?** (Chapter 3)

- Think through **what a death "congenial with your own values" looks like and means to you** (Chapter 4)

- **Expand your thinking about factors that contribute to dying well** by tapping into the wisdom of **others** (either through a book, article, workshop or in person) (Chapter 5)

- Ponder who will be **in charge** at life's end; note your wishes about what you would want and who might help you achieve that in case you are not capable (Chapter 6)

- Reflect on how you want to deal with the possibility of **"slow death"** (Chapter 7)

- List the **developmental tasks** you want to tackle (Chapter 8)

- Consider how to maintain **communication** if it becomes difficult for you (Chapter 9)

- **Identify steps you want to take to prepare for a thoughtful death** and any **hurdles** you see in taking those steps (Chapter 10)

- Contemplate **family patterns** regarding death and how they influence what you want (Chapter 11)

- "Have a **circle of intimates** to be with you so death is not solitary" are Arnold's words. Is this something you are open to? (Chapters 4 and 12)

- How do you respond to the suggestion that "you can take an **off ramp**"? (Chapter 13)

- Reflect on **how your death could be a gift to others.** (Chapter 14)

- Would **reflection over time** on "befriending death" enhance your thinking? (Chapter 15)

- Which **"light keepers"** keep you company as you ponder life's completion? (Chapter 16)

This is intended as a review, not a "to do" list. These items occurred to me over a thirty-year period as I explored what seemed important at the time. Go where your energy leads you. Simply setting aside a container or a notebook for ideas might be a place to begin. Hopefully, *Looking Forward* has awakened you to possibilities. As you pay attention to life as it evolves, you'll come across insights, people and tools that might have special meaning as you find your personal way to enrich the end of life.

For Further Reading

Albom, Mitch. *Tuesdays with Morrie: an old man, a young man, and life's greatest lesson.* **New York: Doubleday, 1997.** *The story of Mitch's visits with his mentor as Morrie lives his last days with humor, originality, and soul. A personal view of how one person experiences and shapes his own death.*

Bernardin, Joseph Cardinal. *The Gift of Peace: Personal Reflections.* **Chicago: Loyola Press, 1997.** *An intimate look at how Cardinal Bernardin, faced with a limited time to live, opened himself more fully to God through prayer and found "God's special gift to us all: the gift of peace."*

Booth, Janet. *Re-Imagining the End of Life: Self-Development & Reflective Practices for Nurse Coaches,* **2019.** *This concise, clear handbook provides tools and reflective questions to explore personal beliefs about aging, advanced illness, and dying as a way to enrich life's end for oneself and those close to us. Although written for nurses, these tools can help anyone bring compassionate presence to the experience of life's end.*

Borysenko, Joan. *Pocketful of Miracles.* **New York: Warner Books, 1994.** *Practices from the world's wisdom traditions offer training in living with heart and depth. Three of us used this* *for eight years and experienced incredible soul nourishment and bonding with each other.*

Butler, Katy. *Knocking on Heaven's Door: The Path to a Better Way of Death.* **New York: Scribner, 2013.** *The riveting story of how the author and her parents faced death and confronted wrenching moral questions. When does death stop being a curse and become a blessing? Where is the line between saving a life and prolonging a death? When do you say to a doctor, "Let my loved one go"? Contemplating the lack of peace she felt with her mother's death, the author writes with refreshing honesty, "We had done our best. We had expressed, in our own peculiar and broken ways, our love. She had not been a perfect mother. I had not been a perfect daughter. It had not been a perfect death. I would never live a perfect life."*

Butler, Katy. *The Art of Dying Well: A Practical Guide to a Good End.* **New York: Scribner, 2019.** *The author writes, "People who are willing to confront their aging, vulnerability, and mortality often live better lives in old age and illness and experience better deaths, than those who don't. They keep shaping lives of comfort, joy, and meaning, even as their bodies decline." This book presents the bases to cover and the resources available to thrive, even in the face of disappointment and adversity, as people prepare for their final days.*

Byock, Ira. *Dying Well: Peace and Possibilities at the End of Life.* **New York: Riverhead Books, 1997.** *I love the way Dr. Byock presents the spiritual aspect of dying with stories and language that are accessible to all – those convinced of the value of spirit and those who question it.*

Byock, Ira. *The Four Things That Matter Most: A Book About Living.* **New York: Simon & Schuster, Inc., 2004.**

These four things (forgiving, receiving forgiveness, loving, and thanking) can bring so much richness to the one who is dying and those who are close to the person.

Byock, Ira. *The Best Care Possible: A Physician's Quest to Transform Care Through the End of Life.* **New York: Penguin Group, 2012.** *Dr. Byock, through compelling stories, elucidates how those involved can bring the best care to each dying person. He also provides vivid examples of how entire communities and society can be mobilized to bring beauty, spirit, and sensitive hands-on support for the dying.*

Chodron, Pema. *Comfortable With Uncertainty.* **Boston: Shambala Publications, 2002.** *Buddhist practices distilled in bite-sized chunks. "Difficulties are the path," states Pema Chodron. This book invites us to engage in specific practices to walk that path with grace.*

de Hennezel, Marie. *Intimate Death: How the dying teach us to live.* **New York: Alfred A. Knopf, 1997.** *The story of how a gifted French psychotherapist encourages those who are dying to live each remaining day as fully as possible. She writes, "Death has been my daily companion for years, and I refuse to trivialize it. It has given me the most intense experiences of my life...I cannot deny the suffering and sometimes the horror that surround death...But alongside this suffering, I feel I have been enriched, that I've known moments of incomparable humanity and depth that I would not exchange for anything in the world, moments of joy and sweetness incredible as that may seem."*

de Hennezel, Marie. *The Art of Growing Old: Aging with Grace.* **New York: Viking, 2010.** *A quote from Abbe Pierre, a well-known French priest, begins this book: "We must always keep both eyes open: one eye on the world's suffering so that we can fight* *against it, and the other on its wondrous beauty so that we may give thanks for it." This book describes the author's turnaround: "I had to go to the heart of the suffering and fear that the experience of growing old generates in order to understand everything it has to offer in terms of human and spiritual enrichment." Some vital elderly people in Okinawa, the "Island of Long Life" helped her see that their radiance was very much "the fruit of deliberate, clear-headed work." She shares her discoveries about turning our advancing years into "a fulfilling adventure, a time of growth...a youthfulness of heart."*

duBoulay, Shirley. *Cicely Saunders: The Founder of the Modern Hospice Movement*. London: Hodder and Stoughton Limited, 1984. *A sensitive picture of the life and thinking of a person who brought heart, companionship, uniquely effective symptom relief, and her own presence to the profound experience of dying.*

Dunn, Hank. *Hard Choices For Loving People*. Lansdowne, VA: A & A Publishers, 1990. *A chaplain explains medical end-of-life decisions and choices for families and patients. Most reassuring at the end of this short, informative guide, Hank Dunn shares his personal views on the meaning of the choices we face – the emotional and spiritual challenge of letting go and letting be.*

Frankl, Victor E. *Man's Search for Meaning*. Boston: Beacon Press, 1946 (Vienna, Austria); 1959 (United States). *A psychiatrist's chronicle of his experiences as a prisoner in a Nazi concentration camp during World War II and his therapeutic method that involved identifying a positive purpose in life and then imaging the outcome. Two famous quotes: "Those who have a 'why' to live, can bear with almost any 'how'." "Everything can be taken from a man but one thing: the last of the human freedoms – to* choose one's attitude in any given set of circumstances, to choose one's own way."

Gawande, Atul. *Being Mortal: Medicine and What Matters in the End.* **New York: Henry Holt and Company, 2014.** *Writing as a son, son-in-law, and doctor, the author describes what medical practice offers the dying and also medicine's limitations. The book is laced with stories of people living to the last with autonomy, dignity, and joy.*

Harrington, Samuel. *At Peace: Choosing a Good Death After a Long Life:* **New York: Grand Central Life and Style, 2018.** *Learning from his father's death, Dr. Harrington discusses how to avoid too much technology and embrace compassionate care at life's end. He encourages readers to decline aggressive treatment, embrace hospice care, and create a vision of their own death.*

Kiernan, Stephen P. *Last Rights: Rescuing the End of Life From the Medical System.* **New York: St. Martin's Press, 2006.** *Presents stories of people who lived life fully right up to the last moment. The author offers a profound vision for patients, doctors, and families to honor the dying, to maintain meaningful connections, and to approach dying with ultimate respect.*

McCullough, Dennis. *My Mother, Your Mother: Embracing "Slow Medicine," The Compassionate Approach to Caring For Your Aging Loved Ones.* **New York: HarperCollins Publishers, 2008.** *Imagine having a wise doctor, experienced friend, caring family member, and sensitive spiritual teacher at your side as you journey through your own last days or those of a loved one. That is what it is like to read this comprehensive and sensitive book.*

Nouwen, Henri J. *Our Greatest Gift: A Meditation on Dying and Caring.* New York: Doubleday and Company, Inc., 1994. *Determined to learn to befriend death, the author discovered also how his death could be a gift for others.*

Ostaseski, Frank. *The Five Invitations: Discovering What Death Can Teach Us About Living Fully.* New York: Flatiron, 2017. *Insights, soulful perspective, and practical guidance distilled from a lifelong experience with death and dying. Several of the most skillful and compassionate individuals called to help people die well have studied with Ostaseski. His book enables the rest of us to learn from a master.*

Parr, Carolyn Miller and Cohen, Sig. *Love's Way: Living Peacefully With Your Family As Your Parents Age.* Peabody, Massachusetts: Hendrickson Publishers, 2019. *Written by two family mediators, this practical and well-organized guide helps families tackle end of life questions in an open way.*

Remen, Rachel Naomi. *Kitchen Table Wisdom: Stories That Heal.* New York: Riverhead Books, 1996. *Both this book and the book listed below consist of stories from the author's experience as a person coping with chronic illness as well as a doctor/counselor/healer helping people find their way to healthy ways of living, having a disease, and dying.*

Remen, Rachel Naomi. *My Grandfather's Blessings. Stories of Strength, Refuge, and Belonging.* New York: Riverhead Books, 2000. *As I mentioned in the text, I want Dr. Remen's books at my side for my journey at life's end. I hope that family members and friends who are present will appreciate these stories with me to call forth our very best in this most important life transition.**

Sacks, Oliver. *Gratitude.* **New York: Alfred A. Knopf, Inc., 2015.** *The four essays mentioned in the text were published in this book. Sacks explores his feelings about completing life and coming to terms with death. "My predominant feeling is one of gratitude. I have loved and been loved. I have been given much and I have given something in return. Above all, I have been a sentient being, a thinking animal, on this beautiful planet, and that in itself has been an enormous privilege and adventure."*

Sarton, May. *A Reckoning.* **New York: W. W. Norton & Company, 1981.** *The protagonist of this novel, Laura Spelman, faced with a terminal illness, wants "to have my own death." For her, this means solitude to "float" and "think my own thoughts" and tender communion with those with whom she has had a "real connection."*

Schachter-Shalomi, Zalman and Ronald S. Miller. *From Age-ing to Sage-ing: A Profound New Vision of Growing Older.* **New York: Warner Books, Inc., 1995.** *This useful book presents historical perspectives and practical tools to help elders become mentors in the family and the wider world, and finally to approach death consciously as an opportunity for spiritual awakening.*

Schwalbe, Will. *The End of Your Life Book Club.* **New York: Vintage Books, 2012.** *During her chemotherapy appointments, a mother and her son discuss the books they love and how they make sense of life. Both Will Schwalbe and Mary Anne Schwalbe find a unique way to have fun, share deeply, and utterly transform what many would only see as a painful slide downhill. Being creative with the last days of life can bring unexpected discoveries, delight, and awakening for those who choose to forge their own path.*

Yungblut, John. *On Hallowing One's Diminishments.* **Wallingford PA: Pendle Hill Publications, 1990.** *Devastated that he had contracted Parkinson's Disease, the author remembered a phrase from his favorite author, Pierre Teilhard de Chardin, "hallowing one's diminishments." Consulting the dictionary, for the word "hallow", Yungblut discovered these meanings: "consecrate, make holy, respect greatly." This 27-page booklet describes his journey of learning how to respect, consecrate, and hallow a physical condition that was most unwelcome. I consult it regularly when my own diminishments call forth the need for "hallowing".*

*In recent correspondence, Dr. Remen updated me on her work: "My work at present is in protecting health professionals from burnout by enabling Physicians, Nurses, Veterinarians, Physician Assistants, Hospice Workers the opportunity to experience their daily work not as a job or a science but in an older way…as a Calling, a Practice, and an act of Service…three spiritual words from Medicine's deep past that have been used to describe the essential nature of this work for thousands of years. My Institute, The Remen Institute for the Study of Health and Illness (RISHI) offers courses for professionals at all levels of training. The Healer's Art, the course I developed almost three decades ago for first year medical students, has been taught at more than one hundred medical schools here and abroad, and some 25,000+ medical students have completed it. (This is what I will probably lead with when I finally meet St. Peter at the heavenly gates.)"

A BIG THANKS

Many thanks go to everyone mentioned in the text. Learning from their experience and wisdom has been totally enriching. Their fortitude and depth in exploring what can be a tough subject is inspiring.

My husband, Dave, and our son and daughter, Tom and Peg, took time they really didn't have to read the text carefully and offer many suggestions. Input from them has been crucial for me. Their spouses, Mary McMakin and Frank Marshall, have given them and me much appreciated support and feedback.

When I mentioned to Barbara "Bim" Werle the idea of writing about death preparation, she said, "Let's do it!" Her enthusiastic willingness to think things through with me was the shove needed to get busy and write. Barbara Greene, nearing the end of life, asked me to read her every line. Her excellent suggestions have been incorporated in the text. Friends Claudia Rose, Mary Catharine Jones, Craig Smith, Zail Berry, Claire Trazenfeld, and Fran Stoddard have also offered encouragement and ideas. Virginia friends, Ricci and Dee Waters, have shared their thoughts and (oh, so important!) computer help.

My friend in Normandy, Brigitte LeColley, in order to share the text with her friends, labored with enthusiasm to prepare a French translation. Irene Rachat, a new friend here and a native French speaker, spent much time listening to the meaning of what I was trying to share in English and then being sure that was expressed in the translation, *Perspectives d'avenir: Le parcourse en plenitude d'une personne avec la mort pour compagne.*

How empowering it is to have these thoughtful people contributing wisdom and companionship on this most important journey. Thanks to you all!

ABOUT THE AUTHOR

My life has been devoted to imagining how life could be better and figuring out steps to achieve that. Arenas of action have been family, work, spirituality, and organizations. This question is always there for me: How can we do our best, be creative, and contribute to a flourishing planet? It seems natural to look at death in the same way.

In his book *From Age-ing to Sage-ing* (1995), Rabbi Zalman Schlachter-Shalomi writes that one role for elders is "to mentor the world." Through my work as a vocational counselor and organizational consultant and my life as a family member and friend, mentoring is something I have loved giving and receiving. But how to mentor the world that seems headed in questionable directions? When I heard that the road near our home in Virginia was going to be widened to sixteen lanes, my heart sank. "We're going to pave over the whole earth," I thought. But other messages particularly from global thinker, Lester Brown, were getting through. He insists that we have all the knowledge and tools needed to restore planetary health and a flourishing world civilization. Furthermore, these tools have already been tried successfully in places around the world.

At a workshop, Elsa Porter, former Assistant Secretary of Commerce, introduced herself, "The world is heading either for disaster or a global renaissance. I'm putting my life behind a global renaissance." My immediate response was that I wanted to do that too. This set me on a path. I devoted a year to researching what one person could do to help produce a Global Renaissance. Conclusions reached are summarized in a booklet, *Our Defining Moment: A Call to Create the World We Truly Want* (2008).

When we retired to Vermont, people asked what I would be doing to foster Global Renaissance. Honestly, I had no clue. Then through some serendipitous events that happened during the first week, I met two experienced Vermonters who wanted to read my booklet. Afterwards, they said, "We would like to do something with this."

We helped organize a network of organizational leaders doing significant sustainable development work overseas. Each leader has a dream related to a piece of Global Renaissance, such as pure water for the world, healthy families, and bringing down the population rate. All are putting their lives and work behind their dreams. You can learn more at: www.vermontglobalexchange.org. *Our Defining Moment* is posted there.

Through this involvement, I have learned that at every moment there is a choice: Will we be reactive or creative? It seems natural to ponder the question: How can I, given the cards I've been dealt, be creative at the end of life so that my dying time might bring blessing to others and myself?

EPILOGUE

Looking Forward was first written in 2018. Some hard copies were circulated. Readers were generous with their appreciation.

A year later, Dave was diagnosed with MDS (myelodysplastic syndrome) which meant his bone marrow was not producing healthy cells. Not much is known about how to treat this. His days were numbered. We just didn't know how many he had! This meant our world shrank. No more adventures or travels. Suddenly we were in the Land of Uncertainty. Not that we were alone. This all happened just about the time COVID hit. The challenge was to learn helpful tools to deal well with our new situation. Dave began building a vertical garden, something he had long wanted to do. We soaked in the love, good wishes and prayers that came our way.

Dr. Zail Berry had said she had never seen "a good death" happen without preparation. Our family took this to heart.

The work we did with this book had put us on the same page. Dave's strong decision-making skills made things doable. When a question came up, he decided the next step quickly and confidently. This brought peace to us. His last decision was to move with me to our local hospice residence called Respite House. Our final days were spent in great tranquility with superlative care in this loving place. Much time was spent outside enjoying the fall colors and fresh air as well as calling family members.

Dave died in his sleep at Respite House on October 10, 2021. It was a peaceful end to a full life. Both of us were 87. Since his death, I have been learning to do the chores he did so competently, organizing our affairs, and pondering how my last days will play out. A question now is: What will I leave behind? Since working with this book has meant so much to our family and friends, I wanted to share it more widely.

It has been a joy to collect photos of the people I wrote about. They highlight what is obvious. The presence of wise, knowledgeable, and caring people brings immeasurable richness to the death experience.

One of the greetings we received during Dave's illness was from Case Pieterman, who enclosed this photo of us. It brought to mind a quote we had read years ago which captured our approach to life and also to death:

"Love does not consist in gazing at each other, but
in looking outward in the same direction."

Antoine de Saint-Exupéry

Made in the USA
Middletown, DE
12 August 2022

71241855R00054